A Soul Protected

Cult Survival and Recovery from PTSD

Valerie Martin, MSEd, CYT

Copyright © 2013 Valerie Martin, MSEd, CYT
All Right Reserved.

ISBN: 1494241927
ISBN 13: 9781494241926

For my children
And for our families, who suffered with us

The names and locations in this account
have been changed to protect the privacy of former members.

Contents

	Prologue	vii
	Introduction	ix
1.	The Setup	1
2.	Entrapment	5
3.	No Escape	11
4.	Parking Lots and Swimming Pools	15
5.	The Queen of Heaven	19
6.	Isolation	21
7.	Ash Fork	23
8.	Yavapai	27
9.	California Dreamin'	31
10.	Nolo Contendere	33

11. Walking Away	37
12. Angels Unawares	41
13. Broken Bits	43
14. Recovery	47
15. Restoration	51
16. Dan, Jason, and Christine	59
17. Healing Tools	63
18. The Empowering and Transformational Power of Prayer, Meditation and Yoga	69
19. Practice, Practice, Practice	73
Acknowledgments	79
About the Author	81
Bibliography	83

Prologue

This book was written in four stages. The first stage, the Introduction, was an investigation I designed to help me understand what factors set the stage for the events described here.

The second stage consisted of unburdening myself of emotions by recounting significant events—both those I felt victimized by and those I felt complicit in. This was an extremely important part of my recovery from PTSD, and it was necessary to make the time as well as seek professional support to engage in this process. I believe many of us suffer from traumatic events that have deeply wounded us. These events could be betrayal by a family member; physical, sexual, or mental/emotional abuse; abortion, incest, and illness; loss of a loved one; war; or a debilitating physical injury. In our efforts to "soldier on," we frequently ignore the need to heal these psychic wounds. We try to push them away, but in fact, they are only buried, and the result is that our lives become shaped and defined by them in ways so subtle we are often unaware of the damage they create.

The third stage reflects the knowledge I have gained through the practice of prayer, meditation and yoga. These practices, in addition to telling my story completely, have enabled me to experience a newfound freedom, unburdened by much of the past and growing ever more whole. The fourth stage is the final chapter in which I outline the daily practices that are required to make lasting changes in behavior, thought and emotional patterns. I cite resources that you may find helpful in your own journey, and I offer you this roadmap for healing from whatever trauma you have suffered. You can transform your life into one of greater joy, peace, and compassion for yourself and others.

Namaste.

Introduction

The source of my trauma was involvement with what has been called an aberrational Christian cult, meaning its teachings were an aberration of the true teachings of Christ. In it, my family was brutalized physically and emotionally.

In 1979, my husband and I, along with our two children, ages eight and eleven, joined the Living Waters. It was a time when many religious, alternative communities were popular. The Hari Krishna were in all the airports, members of the Unification Church (Mooneys) were making headlines, and the shocking tragedy of Jonestown, in which all church members had been coerced into committing suicide, had just been uncovered. Of course, my family and I did not consider ourselves to be involved in anything as radical and dangerous as that.

The Living Waters appeared to be a Christian ministry—I first encountered its members through a Bible study group in our town. They were engaged in a healing ministry—in the healing of memories. Each meeting began with a session of song and inspiration. The leader's wife was a talented pianist and singer; the music was stirring and set a mood for worship and receptivity. There were two main families in the group at that time—Robert and Michelle Damen and Bud and Francis Carter. They each had three children, ranging in age from eight to nineteen. The rest of the group consisted of young single men and women: Edwin, Steven, Janet, Susan, Cora, Michael, and Jane. All the members lived as a community in two homes in neighboring California communities. The group had originated in Texas. The Carters had left a successful farming business. I'm not sure what Robert Damen did before he received his calling as an "apostle" (he might have been a used car salesman). When Robert described his conversion and calling experience, he described being depressed and completely isolated in a darkened room—I wonder now if this was a psychic break. I don't believe in minimizing people's spiritual experience, but we can judge everything by its fruit. In this case, the "Living Waters" were actually "Poison Waters" to everyone, with the possible exception of Robert—and I'm not even sure that it was a positive experience for him. In any event, together the two families had forsaken all to "follow Christ" in the uncompromising gospel that Robert taught.

This story is one of entrapment, coercion, physical, mental, emotional, and spiritual devastation, and finally, recovery and restoration. The devastation wrought by this group took place in a brief twenty-two-month period, but the healing took more than three decades. What were the seeds that allowed two intelligent people such as my husband and me to be deceived and to accept, albeit with difficulty, the doctrine of this man? How could we have put our children and ourselves at such risk? What factors were in play as the experience spiraled out of control? How did we accept the abuse—abuse of the type that we have seen played out repeatedly in groups such as the Branch Davidians, Heaven's Gate, and lesser-known groups around the world? These are questions I sought to answer for myself and for anyone else who may gain insight from them.

The following chapters describe the worst of my memories; they are probably somewhat out of chronological order due to the length of time passed, and there are certainly others I could recount, but these carry the most pain, shame and guilt. I want to make it clear that I do not blame my parents, Dan's parents, Catholicism, or Dan for any of the events that took place in the Living Waters. I am merely attempting to describe the conditions that existed in us and in our relationship that made us prey to Robert's deception. And this is my story. This is what I experienced. Other cult survivors, including Dan and the children, have their own stories, and their survival is also a testimony to God's grace and the resilience of the human spirit. I have not been able to interact with other former cult members who shared this experience with me, though a few reached out. I make no apologies; it was simply too painful.

Further, I believe all the people who followed Robert Damen were sincere and meant no harm to one another, having a true desire to know and follow God. However, as we abandoned ourselves to Robert and his teachings, we lost our selves and became complicit in the destruction of one another. The children were the ultimate victims..

one

The Setup

I thought I was following God—this is the mantra I have repeated over and over in my mind during the past thirty years. When I first got out of the cult I was angry with God—*How could you let this happen? I trusted you! Why did you do this to me?* As I reflected over the years, I discovered there were other forces driving me—Yes, I had wanted to follow God, and perhaps my ideas about how to do that had been misguided. All had involved sacrificing everything, or most everything, for Christ's sake. I had grown up enthusiastically reading the lives of the saints, and being a good Catholic meant being good and suffering—avoiding sin and the near occasion of sin. This is not to say I avoided all sin, but I developed a strong scrupulosity, and thus a lot of shame and guilt-based feelings heading into adulthood. According to Rev. Thomas M. Santa, CSSR, in his essay "Scrupulosity and How to Overcome It," the scrupulous person has a negative image of God, and the key to understanding it may lie in the childhood experiences of the individual—rigid or repressive teachings from authority figures, in the home and out of it, contribute to the condition.

John Gottman, PhD, in his book *The Relationship Cure*, speaks of our "emotional heredity"—what we learned about ourselves from our families of origin. He says that every family has an emotional philosophy they practice and that shapes their members. A family can be emotionally dismissing, emotionally disapproving, laissez-faire, or emotionally coaching. Children (or adults) can learn that their feelings are not important and have no relevance (dismissing); that their feelings are bad or incorrect and should be changed (disapproving); that their feelings "just are," and the individual is provided no counsel as to how to manage them (laissez faire); or that their feelings can present learning situations that can be managed and can enhance growth and maturity (emotional coaching, the optimal emotional philosophy.)

My family of origin was a family of dismissal and disapproval. "Keep crying and I'll give you something to cry about"; "Stop being such a baby!"; "You're so selfish—who do you think you are?"; "You shouldn't feel that way." All were common phrases in my household when negative emotions arose. To complicate matters further, my mother had been diagnosed with paranoid schizophrenia. Her reality was not the reality shared by the rest of the family. You can imagine how confusing this was for me as a child. My father was a good man, but a man ill equipped to handle the complexities of mental illness and four young children. He wanted order, and he wanted it now. I believe these circumstances and the strict religious doctrine I misperceived set the precedent for discounting my own perceptions and feelings. Good, loving, positive thoughts or forgiving thoughts were only allowed for others—but critical and condemning thoughts were justified for me. I internalized the message that there was something wrong with me if I didn't like a particular circumstance or person. I was being selfish, greedy, and bad.

I learned to negate and be ashamed of my negative feelings rather than to examine and understand them and take appropriate action. This deeply ingrained pattern, along with many misapplied scriptural references such as "Deny yourself, pick up your cross, and follow me," made me the perfect target for Robert's brand of religion.

In addition, my marriage was troubled. My husband drank too much and had a bad temper. It was difficult for me to communicate with him. I felt I had to walk on eggshells all the time since I didn't know what might set him off. He often flew off the handle, sometimes becoming rough with the children. I was really hoping God would change him. My attempts at addressing our marital issues with my husband were met with anger. The year I met the Living Waters ministry, Dan had been involved in a hit-and-run accident in San Clemente while drinking, and this shook him up. No one was harmed, but the event was a catalyst for his interest in the ministry and God in general. He also had participated in a very bitter strike at his workplace. His foundations had been rocked.

I had been hurt deeply by Dan in our marriage. In addition to emotionally and verbally abusing me due to his drinking and temperament, he had begun telling me during our first year together that he was in love with one of his senior high school students. I had been his student too, and although he had never expressed his feelings for me until after I graduated, I had not anticipated that I would be the first in a string of "loves." I was completely knocked off balance by learning that he was in love with another woman. At eighteen, with a new baby, I hardly knew what to make of my situation. I pretty much felt "I had made my own bed," so as a Catholic, I resigned myself to accepting his infidelity. To say I was dazed and confused by it all would have been an understatement. You can imagine my humiliation; I had no one to turn to.

Since my family, though loving and well intentioned, had not provided me with a solid example of marriage or parenting (through no fault of their own), and since I carried a long list of religious requirements, I did not possess a compass for "normal." Dan's family had been plagued by alcoholism, and though they deeply loved him, he was no more equipped than I was at finding "true north."

When we first met members of the Living Waters, they were warm and welcoming. Everyone was kind and loving. We felt safe to express our flaws and shortcomings in the face of what seemed to be God's unconditional love. Our flaws, though, were then used as wedges to isolate us from one another, turn us against each other, and coerce us to stay when we wanted to leave, or simply bring us into line. Shame and guilt became powerful tools, and we gave our fellow cult members plenty of material. As my brother Craig would say, "We loaded the gun."

two

Entrapment

Our visits and early days at the ranch in the Mojave Desert of California were idyllic. There was a swimming pool and horses to ride, and our children, Jason and Christine, quickly made friends their own ages. Dan and I enjoyed the worship services and communal meals shared with good-natured camaraderie.

The ranch had been a former dude ranch. It was in the shape of a U, with the common living room, dining room, and kitchen at one end, individual rooms with their own bathrooms on one side, and dorm-type rooms on the other. The interior of the U was lined with a covered walkway. The buildings were made of bricks painted white—a very cool material for the desert heat—and the covered walkway kept the heat out as well. In the center was a lawn, and at the end of the lawn was a swimming pool. There were separate quarters where Robert and Michelle stayed. Other families were visiting the ranch and were considering joining as well. We all lived in the Huntington Beach area and had met at the ministry's Bible study, and we came out to visit on weekends.

Robert believed that we were in the "end times," and that he, as an apostle, was led to establish the ministry and ranch as a refuge and teaching center. The ranch was ten acres. There was a plan to build a large meeting room for services and to add a schoolroom. Robert told Dan he would be the pastor and principal of the school and I would teach—something I had always wanted to do. I'm not sure what enticements and titles he offered to the other families. Additional buildings would be added to the compound as people came to the ranch for counseling or schooling or joined the ministry. The ranch would be self-sufficient, raising its own food. *Wow, this all sounded pretty good.* And there was already so much in place—the plan didn't seem far-fetched.

There was a two-acre garden that provided fresh vegetables. Everyone worked in the garden. The women in the ministry blanched the vegetables so they could be frozen and used in the winter. Francis, Bud's wife, was in charge of the kitchen. She was a wonderful southern cook. She planned the meals, and the women and girls assisted in the cooking, serving, and kitchen cleanup. Sunday evenings we just ate sandwiches, so that everyone could relax with their families in the evenings.

Each couple had their own room. The boys and young men shared a dorm, and the girls and single women also shared a dorm. Though I remember this seemed strange to my father, who thought it odd that families weren't housed together, he accepted the housing arrangements since we seemed satisfied. My father even had ideas for installing a large walk-in refrigerator in the kitchen. During our early days in the ministry, families were welcomed for visits. We went home for Thanksgiving and a family funeral that occurred that same month. My mom and her husband came to the ranch for Christmas. The children put on plays and singing performances in the evenings. I remember thinking, "Gee, this is just like the Walton's." Our lifestyle was so homespun and wholesome—everything I was looking for.

It wasn't long before things started deteriorating. We soon became witness to Robert's public shaming and humiliation of ministry members, when it was determined that they were "out of the spirit." This happened regularly and was generally a surprise to the accused party. The "elders in the community," whom scripture says we are to respect, accepted this humiliation as training and discipline. Robert used his confrontational stands as examples of the brethren correcting one another in love—if this wasn't a love we recognized, it was because we were inundated with the false love of the world and didn't understand God's ways.

There were also punishing volleyball games—if you missed the ball, it was because you were out of the spirit, or worse, in a state of rebellion. Not too good for those of us with less athleticism. A few months after we moved to the ranch Robert started turning his cruelty on our son, Jason, and insisting that I take "a stand" with him in order for us both to get free of my idolatry. Obviously, I loved my children too much, Robert insinuated. What I never understood really is why these "stands" had to be so harsh and mean. Can't you just gently tell a child or person that he or she is doing the wrong thing and suggest the preferred alternative? Since many of these offenses took place "in the spirit," there was never any real behavior to point out—this filled all of us with anxiety and kept us hyper vigilant. You never knew if you might be next.

At around the same time, Robert was insisting we take "stands" with friends and relatives—this meant we had to point out their faults and tell them they were going to hell if they didn't convert to Robert's "Gospel." The purpose was to "come out from among them" and demonstrate our true love for them because we were willing to risk their rejection in order that "they too might be saved" (1 Corinthians, 10:33: *For I am not seeking my own good but the good of many, so that they may be saved*).

So many of the scriptures were taken out of context, misinterpreted, or misapplied. But having been raised Catholic, we didn't have a solid foundation in Bible study. We had relied on the church (priests) to interpret the Bible for us in their homilies, so having Robert interpret the scriptures wasn't foreign to us. Hence, we tried to accept the doctrine even though it felt wrong and foreign. For the individual members of the Living Waters, this struggle between what is held dear as a keystone value and the new information, supposedly of God, created more than cognitive dissonance, that feeling of tension that comes from holding two conflicting beliefs at the same time. It created, in my opinion, a psychic tear. More than one of the Living Waters members described feeling as though their bodies and minds were being turned inside out—as with a primal scream. What I observed is that people coped in one of two ways: either they capitulated completely, their perceptions becoming one with Robert's and the cult's doctrines, or they "blew out" and left the ministry temporarily or permanently. A person could not sustain this mental tension for an indefinite period of time.

Years after we had left the cult I realized that if we had listened to our gut feelings during the first few months at the ranch, we could have been out of the ministry before our house in Huntington Beach had sold. This would have been embarrassing for us, I'm sure, but better than staying in. However, Robert's practice of using our flaws against us had already begun to diminish our self-confidence and inner reliance. By playing us against each other, Robert was methodically expanding divisions between us. Ultimately, sharing our concerns about the group candidly with one another became impossible.

Robert was a master manipulator, and he played everyone well. To this day, I'm not sure if he was sincerely deceived or a disturbed sociopath.

three

No Escape

Initially, Dan struggled more than I did within the confines of the cult. He started to doubt the wisdom of joining the ministry. In fact, he was filled with anxiety and lost sleep as the day to move came closer. We would open the Bible at random places, seeking signs and confirmation. Effectively and perhaps in anticipation of converts' doubts, Robert sent one of the young women to stay with us once we had decided to join. This was to help support us, as Satan would try to attack us and get us to change our minds.

Dan said that when he woke up at the ranch the first morning, he had a sick feeling in his stomach and wondered, "What have I done?" But he decided, "I'm just going for it!" He said after we were out that he had agreed to join the group in order to keep the family together. I guess he thought I would go without him. Here's another example of the faulty communication that existed in our relationship, because while I can't say what would have happened if he had refused to go, I can say I was deeply entrenched in the submissive wife-doctrine. Leaving without him would certainly have been a stretch—though who can say what tactics Robert might have used to keep me in? On the other hand, Robert may not have wanted me in the group without Dan. Clearly, without Dan, there would have been no proceeds from the sale of our house and no money from Dan's retirement fund, which Dan cashed out.

A sickening event took place early on at the ranch, while I thought we were waiting for Dan's check to come from the state retirement system. It was to be about $15,000. One day Dan disappeared. He took our Buick and didn't come back for several days. When he returned like the prodigal son, he confessed that he had taken the check and gone to Las Vegas. He had spent all the money on hotels, hookers, and gambling. I didn't blame Dan for this, but I did feel crushed by it, lost, and rejected in the most dramatic way. This was equally devastating to Dan. He was convinced of his depravity, and he spent months shoveling out the animal pens and doing the most menial tasks as his punishment. I still wonder why he didn't take the money and return to get us out of the Living Waters? I'll never know—We never talked about the Las Vegas incident after we got out. Dan is dead now, so I can't ask him what his thoughts or feelings were at the time.

Shortly after Dan's "blowout," Robert sent some of us out on the road. We distributed *The Facts*, the book he and Jane had written, on college campuses in Texas and Oklahoma. It was his version of the gospel. Robert selected the configuration of the teams. We had a couple RVs and stayed in KOA campgrounds. I was sent with the traveling groups. Dan stayed behind shoveling shit.

Several people had already left the group. Among them were Robert's wife, Michelle Damen, as well as Susan Simpson, the woman who stayed with us when we were preparing to leave our home in Huntington Beach and join the ministry. Presumably, they alerted child protective service authorities to the conditions on the ranch. The authorities sent out investigators, who interviewed all the children. Investigators took no action but filed a report. This caused Robert to become even more paranoid. He considered the investigation persecution for the sake of the gospel. He came up with a plan to take the children off the ranch and leave the state, saying it was for their protection. He and Jane, all the children, and a few of the single adults would move. Dan and I, the Carters, and the rest of the single young men would stay and take care of business at the ranch. This was a turning point for my husband and me. Neither Dan nor I liked the idea, and we decided to leave the ministry. We discussed leaving with both the children. Jason wanted to do whatever his dad and I decided. Christine was less certain and was afraid for our spiritual well-being if we left.

Dan and I told Robert of our decision, and that brought a reversal of roles for Dan and me in the cult. Robert had all the men in the group meet with us. They pressed us as to why we wanted to leave, and I blurted out that I thought that some of the things that went on in the ministry were not of God. That was it! I had dared to judge. Robert said that this exposed the whole plot. I had been attacking Dan in the spirit all along; he wasn't guilty of "blowing out"—it was my fault, and I was behind it because of my idolatry for the children, in particular, Jason. I can't help but think that these accusations must have provided some relief for Dan, as he was no longer the black sheep. The men yelled at me and rebuked Satan relentlessly. I prayed silently and said, "OK, God, if this is what you want, I'll do it. If Dan decides to stay, we'll stay."

Dan did decide to stay, and Robert and Jane took the children the next morning. Now I was the one under suspicion, wavering in my commitment to God and to the ministry. Several months passed. We had word about the children and the camp whenever Michael returned to the ranch for more supplies. He indicated that Christine was doing well, but he referred to Jason as a "Nimrod." Nimrod was a king associated with the biblical Tower of Babel and was known to be rebellious against God. Michael gave no specifics, but I had an uneasy feeling in my stomach that this didn't bode well. We didn't know where the children were; we felt we had no choice but to stay now.

four
Parking Lots and Swimming Pools

Although many memories swirl through my mind, a few retain a vivid quality. One occurred in the parking lot of the ranch before the children were sent off. Robert and Jane were returning from a writing trip to Palm Springs. Robert frequently got away from the ranch because he felt he was being "attacked in the spirit." The bell rang loudly to summon us to join Robert and Jane. I was having a talk with Jason, "taking a stand" in my mind, though quietly. Since "taking a stand" with Jason had become a focus in the ministry, I felt it was best and would be most pleasing to Robert if I finished it. Robert sent someone for us, and as we anxiously arrived at the parking lot, Robert yelled, "Get away from her! Stand back!" All the members—adults and children—did as directed. Numbering thirty-five, they formed a large circle around me in the searing sun. Dust and heat rose from the parking lot, and hot shame rose from inside me.

"Hasn't she tried to seduce all of you? You, George? You, Edwin?" Robert pressed every man and boy loudly, and every man and boy answered in the affirmative that I was guilty of seduction.

I felt like I was the adulteress depicted in the Bible. Surrounded by the angry crowd, gathered to stone her. Except Jesus didn't come to my rescue.

They all began yelling at me and praying in tongues that sounded like a cacophony of curses. George came up and ripped the cross from around my neck and threw it in the dirt at my feet. It was a gift from a dear friend, and I collapsed on my knees in the dirt beside it.

After the verbal stoning, Robert sentenced me to forty days of "sackcloth and ashes." I was not to bathe or change clothes and was to continue with all my regular chores and activities. I was to make myself as unattractive as possible by clipping my hair around my head—Jane helped with this task.

Dazed, I returned to my room. Dan came in and tried to comfort me. I was sweaty and dirty from the dust in the parking lot, hollow inside, with a knot in my chest that wasn't to go away for thirty years. There would be no comfort. As it turned out, my sentence only lasted a few days because a reporter was coming to the ranch and Robert did not want my appearance to be an embarrassment to the ministry.

In the child custody hearings that were to come, as witnesses who were former members described scenes of abuse, Robert was frequently not the person who was named as the perpetrator of the punishment. Someone else was doing the spanking, beating, yelling. However, Robert set the example and standard for every form of punishment. Whether the punishment was laps around the volleyball court, laps around a car, isolation, or beatings with a belt, Robert demonstrated it and pushed members into meting out extreme discipline to avoid punishment themselves. Everything had his tacit approval if not concrete directive.

There was a young man—more or less an outsider—who was in and out of the ministry frequently. He came and went at the ranch, but Robert had not invited him to live there. It happened one night that he had done or not done something that qualified as an offense. Robert threw him into the swimming pool and began choking him and dunking him as he hurled accusations at him. This became the "stand" de rigueur.

I can't remember what my offense was, but I can remember the terror of being thrown into the swimming pool, strangled, and held underwater repeatedly by Dan. He was just doing what he was supposed to do, and hey, it was for my own good anyway. What amazes me as I write this is that it takes so few words to describe such horrific events. In my life it was like watching a train wreck in slow motion; it went on forever. In actuality, it can be described in a few paragraphs.

five
The Queen of Heaven

Robert's gospel contained a revelation concerning "the Queen of Heaven," "the Whore of Babylon," and I became the centerpiece for it. I epitomized the evil spirit of the unsubmitted woman, the Jezebel who sought to destroy men of God. Trent Smith and a few of the other men were to handle the initial confrontation this time. I was called into a meeting with them, and Trent began speaking quietly about an attack on the ministry that was taking place and was caused by an evil spirit from within. It was not unusual to be called out on something there was no awareness of, so I innocently asked, "Is it me?"

"Just like Judas," Trent replied. "Is it I, Lord, who will betray you?" he said mockingly.

It was determined that I would be put in isolation. Robert had purchased a mobile home that had been installed for guests on the side of the main buildings. This is where I was to be sent so I would not contaminate the rest of the group. I was not allowed to see my children or Dan. Cora, one of the single women, brought meals to me—all the while praying vociferously in tongues, so that the spirit would not come into her.

There was to be a "Queen of Heaven Seminar." All of the women and girls were to wear black armbands and maintain silence for the duration of the seminar. Jane was going to do the presentation, and she had prepared materials. One was a poster of a sexily clad woman in a provocative pose. The woman was with a young teen, also provocatively dressed and posed. This was said to be an illustration of Christine and me. I was the Jezebel, training my daughter to be one as well. All of us, women and young girls alike, had to confess to having lust for every man and young boy in the group. It was humiliating. Did we believe it? No, it didn't seem true, but we confessed anyway.

six

Isolation

The first time I was in isolation, I was there about two weeks by myself. I read my Bible and took walks in the desert. If I saw a car from the ministry, I tried to look holy, as if to convince them I was worthy of rejoining the group.

I was allowed out of isolation to attend the Queen of Heaven seminar. Life went on in the ministry. At various times I would hear shouting and rebuking, and one by one the other women in the ministry were sent to isolation with me. Ultimately there were four of us. Sometimes we would talk and read the Bible together. Mostly we were afraid and confused. I remember one evening when we were sitting in the mobile home. All of us were praying and singing. I got a picture in my mind of a cavalry of horses and angels coming to set us free. "I look to the hills from whence cometh my help" (Psalm 121) was the scripture that accompanied the mental image. I'm not sure if I thought it would be a physical or spiritual rescue.

We were released in a few days; I don't know why. I had been in isolation for at least three weeks that time; the other women, for a matter of days to a week. I guess we were to be given a chance to demonstrate that we had learned our lesson and that we would now be submitted to the ministry and to our husbands—which really meant Robert. We lived in terror, never knowing when we might slip up.

Since I had been isolated, I was unaware of all that had taken place in the ministry in my absence. Trent, the man who had called me a Judas, had left the ministry. He had his wife, Joan, kidnapped and deprogrammed, and she was communicating with our family members about the abuse in the group. My brother Phillip showed up at the front gate, but he was not allowed in. He asked if I was OK. I assured him I was—what else would I say? The children were not at the ranch, and I had no idea where they were. Trent Smith sent a policeman to the ranch to ask me if I wanted to leave. Of course I said no. None of this attention from the outside world endeared me to Robert; I was bringing more persecution. Actions against the ministry were intensifying. We were out of money. We were selling things off to meet expenses. The children, a few young adults, and Robert and Jane remained off the ranch

seven

Ash Fork

Of all the chapters I have to write, this is the one of which I'm most ashamed.

When Robert took the children out of state, they ended up in a camping area in Ash Fork, Arizona. We at the ranch didn't know where they were—their location was a secret due to Robert's perceived persecution.

At some point, I was brought to the camp. I think they were allowing Jason to come back into the camp after being isolated. I remember going on a wood-gathering trip with Michael, Jason, and the two boys Jason's age: Drake, who was Robert's son, and Aaron. Something happened on that wood-gathering excursion that prompted Michael to accuse Jason of attacking Drake "in the spirit." These mystical or mythical attacks warranted severe consequences, and this time was no different—except that I was there, and I was the one who was supposed to take the stand with Jason—presumably this would help us break our unholy bond of idolatry. Had they brought me there for this very purpose?

Back at the camp, Michael handed me a belt, and the rest of the camp encircled us. Angry faces surrounded us; among them, Christine's tear-stained face. "Hit him!" they cried over and over, wanting me to take the stand that would "set us free." I looked at them, I looked at the belt in my hand, and I looked at Jason cowering in front of me. My arm was paralyzed. I could not move it at all. After what seemed like hours of this screaming standoff, Robert, with disgust, sent Jason and me to a tent outside the camp. This happened, mind you, within hours of my arrival at the camp, after I had been separated from my children for several months.

I was filled with shame and fear. I knew I must do something to take a stand with Jason—our very lives were in jeopardy. I don't know whether at the time I saw a real spiritual battle or I just wanted to take some action that would, once and for all, put an end to the scapegoating and punishment of Jason and myself. I think it was more the latter, but I can't say I thought it through at that moment.

I started barking orders at Jason to make a path outside our tent, using the rocks that were plentiful in the campground. I yelled and screamed at him and pulled off my tennis shoe to spank him. I did spank him, and his buttocks were deeply bruised. Robert sent someone to tell me to be quiet. I sat with Jason in the tent, humiliated and filled with sorrow—I had failed again.

As we spent the rest of the day and evening there in the tent, I thought about leaving the camp with Jason. But I didn't know where we were, I had no car and no money, and I didn't even know the direction of the highway and what dangers might be out there. And what about Christine? I couldn't leave her there. I couldn't abandon her—she could get punished for my escape, or Robert might use it as another way to drive a wedge between us—"See, your mom doesn't care about you." Again, I saw no options.

I don't remember more than that one day at the camp, so I'm assuming someone took me back to the ranch the following day.

Months passed; Christmas (which we no longer celebrated) came and went. I remember looking up at the dark, starlit sky and feeling the ache in my heart. Though looking at the same sky, my children and I were separated by hundreds of miles. Christmas had been the most important celebration in my family. Gifts, laughter, delicious treats, cooking and baking together created the warmest family memories. What kind of Christmas was this? Did Christine and Jason, isolated from their parents and camping in the desert, feel as bereft as I did?

In Robert's brand of religion, love was hate, and hate was love. Black was white. He used the scripture in Isaiah 55:8—*"For my thoughts are not your thoughts, neither are your ways my ways, said the LORD"*—to convince us that we just didn't understand how God worked. We sure didn't.

eight
Yavapai

To this day, I can't hear the county Yavapai mentioned without shuddering. During the children's stay at the camp in Ash Fork, Arizona, family members who had heard Joan Smith's recounting of the existing abuse planned a rescue of the children in the camp. These family members had also reported the abuse to Arizona authorities. I'm not clear on the sequence of events, but several family members went in search of the group. Finding them involved a chaotic chase through the desert and a simultaneous raid on the camp by authorities, who were able to take Jason into protective custody. I'm not really sure how he was "captured" and the others were not. Dan and I were in California.

Robert and the rest of the entourage returned to the ranch. Jason's custody hearing was to occur in Yavapai, Arizona—that was also where he was in foster care. I cannot imagine what his days were like, but mine were a living hell. There had been a visit arranged for Dan and me to go see Jason before the hearing. Robert and Jane had our good car, and we were left to take Michael's old VW van—it broke down on the way there, and we were unable to get to the visit. We called social services from some bar along the highway, to let them know we had encountered car trouble, but I imagined Jason waiting for us to come and our not showing up—how abandoned he must have felt—how abandoned and alone he and Christine must have felt in the Ash Fork desert. Dan and I got the van running and returned to the ranch in agony.

After the remaining cult members at the Ash Fork camp had returned to the ranch, the children and a few of the younger men had taken to sleeping in sleeping bags in the living room of the ranch, since most of the ranch's furniture and beds had been sold. One night there was a raid on the ranch by about nineteen men, family members and deprogrammers among them. They arrived wearing ski masks and kicking in doors. They were there to kidnap the Wagner family—William, Darla, David, Aaron, and Ruth. We fought them off—I among them—trying to save Aaron from being taken away. They did overpower us and carried the Wagners off in blankets, but something happened—the car broke down or the remaining cult members chased them—I'm not sure which. Somehow the Wagners were "rescued" and returned to the ranch. We were jubilant over God's victory, but within a few days William was in trouble. Robert determined that William had not resisted enough; he had let them carry him and his family away.

The raiders were identified and arrested, including Dan's brother Ronald. They were arraigned and tried. I believe the trial lasted several days. Each of us present for the attempted kidnapping testified as witnesses for the prosecution. All of the raiders were acquitted.

These were among the darkest days for me—a surrealistic haze clouded everything. I waited for the custody hearing in Yavapai, afraid of what would happen. Would we lose Jason? Afraid and feeling guilty, I was blamed repeatedly for the situation. My father was at the hearing, along with Dan's brother and sister-in-law, who wanted custody of Jason. That was the first time I heard all the details about the conditions at Ash Fork and Jason's treatment. The judge's ruling was that although it was a clear case of child abuse, since the group was from California, the case should be under California jurisdiction. Jason was released to us, and of course, Robert and the group felt vindicated, ignoring the judge's words and acting as if the testimony had been considered false. On the ride home in the van, Jason got a ration of verbal abuse from Michael about the new leather jacket that had been purchased for him while in foster care. With a sinking awareness, I knew this was not going to be the end of the abuse for Jason, and I knew I was powerless to defend him.

nine

California Dreamin'

After the custody hearing in Arizona, everyone returned to the ranch. I remember an evening just shortly after Jason's return. We were celebrating our victory with a Mexican feast. The table was laid, and we were gathered in prayer to bless the food, when down the driveway came a string of headlights—ten to fifteen police cars. They came in uniform with lights and cameras. They took movies of the food and the room. This was not too long after Jonestown, so they must have been expecting the worst. They came with orders from child protective services to remove all the children from the ranch. With guards supervising, we tearfully helped the children each pack a bag and get into the police cars. I couldn't believe it. We had just gotten Jason back—now the police were taking all of the children.

As the days unfolded, I became the scapegoat again. I was accused of having caused it all. Robert had his children taken away because of me, or so he claimed. He hired an expensive attorney in Orange County. This law firm frequently represented cult members against family members who were trying to have them removed from similar groups. Robert put the ranch up as collateral for payment. We were in a battle to retain custody of our children; how could we leave now? How distorted our judgment had become—the easiest way to regain our children would have been to renounce the cult and leave. But we couldn't see it; we believed renouncing the cult was the equivalent of renouncing Christ.

Throughout the months that followed, I was in and out of isolation, but mostly in. I searched my Bible and prayed fervently. I was often brought to 1 Corinthians: 13, 1–7.

> *If I speak in the tongues [a] of men or of angels, but do not have love, I am only a resounding gong or a clanging cymbal. 2 If I have the gift of prophecy and can fathom all mysteries and all knowledge, and if I have a faith that can move mountains, but do not have love, I am nothing. 3 If I give all I possess to the poor and give over my body to hardship that I may boast, [b] but do not have love, I gain nothing. 4 Love is patient. Love is kind. It does not envy, it does not boast, it is not proud. 5 It does not dishonor others, it is not self-seeking, it is not easily angered, it keeps no record of wrongs. 6 Love does not delight in evil but rejoices with the truth. 7 It always protects, always trusts, always hopes, always perseveres.*

I measured myself with this standard and knew I was falling short, but was at a loss as to how to improve myself. It occurred to me years later that perhaps God was bringing me to this scripture repeatedly so that I could measure Robert and the ministry with His Word.

ten

Nolo Contendere

The courtroom was lined with dark wood, dark wood everywhere, and windows on the left. Dan and I sat with Russell Meed, the attorney for the cult. Somehow Robert had convinced the attorneys that the removal of all the children from the ministry was persecution and the claims of child abuse were false. Back at the ranch, Robert accused me repeatedly of being culpable for his children being taken away because of my idolatry for mine. The period during the court cases, both in Arizona and California, was agonizing. I remember that everything seemed to be happening in twilight, that rather eerie light that gives you the sense of darkness approaching. From morning to night, it was twilight. I sometimes thought, "I just have to get through this, and have Robert get his children back, and then I can leave and not be blamed for anything anymore."

As Russell advised us that we would plead "no contest" to the allegations of child abuse, my heart sank with the realization that this was really happening. Russell tried to convince us that the plea was not an admission of guilt, but I certainly couldn't see how it wasn't. During the court case in Arizona, which involved only Jason, I had learned some details of the conditions at the camp at Ash Fork. Christine had been placed in a position of complete responsibility for maintaining the camp: cleaning, cooking, and assigning tasks for the other children as well as the adults. She was barely twelve. Michael had been left in charge of meting out the discipline, and he had taken his role seriously.

There were punishing volleyball games in the Arizona heat. Diving for the ball into the sharp desert rocks was commended and the number of cuts and bruises on legs and arms was evidence of the children's dedication to God. Jason, as had become the custom, was the scapegoat for whatever problems existed in the camp—from Robert's son, Drake, wetting his bed, to some perceived "attack in the spirit." Robert and Jane, who had taken the children out of state, were off somewhere writing a book—generally in a hotel—while the rest of the group camped in very primitive conditions. There were others, like Dan and myself, who were back at the ranch. We were to distribute books, do the billing, and maintain the ranch. Until we heard the testimonies in court, Dan and I were unaware of the situation at camp, except through reports that Christine was doing great and Jason was doing poorly. We didn't know about the camp conditions or Jason's repeated isolation from the group.

In court, we learned that Jason had been isolated in a tent by himself outside the camp. Food was brought to him, but he had built his own fire, shared his meals with a rat, and had undergone numerous sessions of verbal humiliation and beatings. He was isolated and shunned by the group except when he was being punished. Christine was forced to be a witness to all this and was not able to intervene in any way. As the story unfolded, the children's treatment was (and still is) horrifying to me. How abandoned and terrified they must have felt. How incomprehensible that anyone could imagine this was God's will.

The end result, after many weeks of hearings and psychological testing for all the adults and children in the group, was that the teenagers and older children were allowed to return if they wanted to. The court's reasoning was that they were old enough to run away if they needed to. I wonder about that. Robert's wife, Michelle, who had left the group, was given custody of their two younger children. The two Wagner boys, who had a mother outside the cult, were returned to her. The baby, Ruth, whose parents both remained in the cult, was in custody of child protective services, as was Jason. The Smiths and their baby had escaped before the children were picked up in California. Joan Smith, who had been kidnapped by her husband and deprogrammed, was the primary witness regarding all that had happened in Ash Fork, including the spanking of babies. She shocked and silenced the courtroom with her description of diapers that exploded after spankings with belts, and wooden spoons.

Once I had left the group, I too became a witness in the remaining custody hearing for Ruth. I testified that Robert's example would determine the discipline that parents and other group members would adopt because "obsequious obedience" was required. Everyone knew that if you didn't take the hardest "stand" possible against the devil in other people (including babies—e.g., if you couldn't control their crying), you would be the next person to be disciplined. I knew that other parents would not be able to make independent decisions in their child rearing, just as I hadn't been. The fact that I participated in this mistreatment of children has been a great source of shame and sorrow for me, and the main contributing factor in the loss of my self-worth.

True, during the Nazi regime and in Darfur, in Liberia, there were similar examples of this behavior, where children were forced to kill others or be killed, and this behavior occurs everywhere where man's inhumanity to man is exemplified by victims victimizing each other. Rampant? Yes. A human commonality? Yes. But nonetheless, shameful and unforgivable. Throughout the years following the cult, I told myself repeatedly, "If I had been a better person, a stronger person, I would not have allowed this to happen." The mantle of guilt and shame felt deserved, and was unbearable.

eleven
Walking Away

The day I walked away from the Living Waters Ranch was a moment I will not forget. Christine had been returned to the ranch because she was old enough to make a choice, and she chose to return. The alternative was the foster care system, some choice. Robert had managed to ruin her homecoming by accusing me of some offense and alienating us as soon as she stepped out of the car. Jason was still in foster care in the custody of the state.

I was in isolation again, but because there was a supervised visit with Jason scheduled, I was in the kitchen with Robert and Jane, and they were talking to me about my visitations with Jason. Robert was telling me that it would be better to lose Jason to the state and ultimately to adoption than for both of us to be damned for eternity due to my idolatry. Jane began singing "in the spirit." At first it was a lovely melody; I began to cry and said to God, "OK, if this is what you want…" Jane's voice began to turn to an ugly, shrieking, condemning one—as it usually did—and I felt a wall go up and a thought crystallize: "I understand if I deserve to be punished for my sins by losing my son, but how is an eight-year-old supposed to make sense of being abandoned by his parents? What did he do?" And then with startling clarity another thought came—"Even if Jason and I are everything they say we are—evil, idolaters, dogs returning to our vomit, or the devil incarnate—THEY'RE NOT RIGHT!"

I didn't think about it any further; I went back to my dorm room, picked up my Bible, and walked off the ranch. I often took walks in the desert and this was not prohibited, so I knew they wouldn't stop me. I walked up main streets, not sure how far. I didn't really know where I was going. I stopped at a house to ask if I could use the phone—it turned out to be the home of people who had recently visited the ranch and who were thinking of joining the ministry. I had silently prayed that day that even though it was my calling to be in the ministry, it wasn't theirs.

They let me use their phone, and I called my mom to come and get me. I waited at their house until she arrived. Without much discussion, she took me to her home. During our time in the cult, the families of cult members had taken different tactics as things went from bad to worse and they heard of the abuse going on. Family members had banded together and hired an attorney and deprogrammer. There were raids on the ranch to kidnap the Wagner family. My dad had spent $10,000 in efforts to get us out and get custody of the children. While the predominant practice was to deny us money when we called asking for financial help from friends and family members, my mom would from time to time send small amounts of cash to me. Though this was frustrating to other family members because this was not the plan, it gave me an ally on the outside—someone I could call—everyone else was the enemy at this point.

During my days at my mom's, I was filled with inner turmoil. "I am like a dog returning to its own vomit"—a scripture Robert used frequently—was one of the thoughts that tortured me. "I am dammed and Jason will be damned with me."

I cannot remember all the battling thoughts that went through my mind, though they lasted for weeks. I didn't call a deprogrammer or James Alloy, the attorney for the families. I did call the attorney who represented the cult members and told him I had left the ministry. I also called the social worker who was handling the cases of the children—Marion, a former nun. She was on vacation in Ventura with her niece and nephew, but in an act of great kindness, she agreed to see me. I drove to Ventura and met with her; with sobs of remorse, I told her my story and of my desire to start putting my family back together and get Jason out of foster care. She believed me and arranged a visit for me at the office of the therapist we had been court ordered to see for family therapy. Marion brought Jason, and my heart broke as I told him how sorry I was for everything that had happened to him. I told him that everything that had been said about him and done to him was wrong. It sickens me to this day. We both cried and embraced. He blew me away when he said, "Robert's books are right, Mom, but he ain't."

The family members and their attorney thought the whole thing was a ruse. They thought I was going to get custody of Jason and then I would run back to the cult and we would all leave the state. Fortunately for me, Marion believed me and arranged an unsupervised weekend visit for me. The story of that weekend and God's intervention on the trip back to Mojave is more evidence of God's grace and protection.

twelve

Angels Unawares

*Be not forgetful to entertain strangers: for thereby
some have entertained angels unawares.*
—Hebrews 13:2

Jason was in foster care with Arlene and Gerry Sure. They were a wonderful couple with a large family and several foster children, including Ruth Wagner. They had a large home outside of Mojave.

The people who lived in the house from which I had called my mom arranged for me to borrow an old Studebaker while I was reestablishing myself and traveling to and from San Bernardino for the child custody hearings and to Mojave to visit Jason and Christine. Our social worker had arranged for supervised visits in the therapist's office.

I planned a couple days at Ventura Beach. There was a Holiday Inn right on the boardwalk. Jason and I were a little shy with each other at first because Robert had accused us of idolatry and shamed us by insinuating that we had an Oedipal attachment. Those anxieties and fears fell away as we enjoyed the sun and ocean and were able to be with one another again, without the fear of scrutiny and reprisal.

I knew we had to be back at the Sures' promptly, to assuage any concerns that I was going to run away with Jason and go back to the cult. In the middle of the desert, on a road not heavily travelled, the Studebaker got a flat tire. There was no spare, and if there had been, I wouldn't have known how to fix it. These were the days before cell phones. I had no way to call for help or reach the Sures to let them know what had happened. I stood next to the car in the desert heat panicking.

An elderly couple in an old station wagon pulled over. The man got out, assessed the trouble, jacked up the car, and removed the tire. He drove Jason and me to the nearest gas station. Not only did he get the tire repaired, he drove us back to our car and put the tire back on. While I was at the station, I was able to use the pay phone and let the Sures know what had happened and the approximate time we'd be back. As I tearfully expressed my appreciation for the couple's kindness and asked how I could repay them, the man said, "Just help someone else when you can."

I remember that ride in their station wagon—no air conditioning, windows open, dust flying, the kindness of strangers, two wizened desert folk—didn't get their names or address—and still thank God for them today.

thirteen

Broken Bits

*Humpty Dumpty sat on a wall; Humpty
Dumpty had a great fall—
All the king's horses and all the king's men
Couldn't put Humpty Dumpty back together again.*

The cult experience was soul shattering; it was as if I had been blown into tiny pieces in that parking lot and all the bits had been carried away, swirling in a flurry above me on the desert winds. My faith in God was shattered. My faith in myself was shattered. Everything I thought and believed was stripped away from me. I couldn't attend church anymore. All the scriptures the priest read or the pastor spoke were the same ones that Robert had used to manipulate, control, and condemn us. Everything I had been trying to fix in my family—alcohol abuse, angry scenes, fear—I received tenfold in the cult. I felt confused and disoriented, startled. What had started out to be an experience bright with hope and inspiration was devastating.

When my family left the cult, we each had a box of clothes. We also had about $12,000 in debt from the ministry's use of our credit cards. All our furniture and household goods had been sold off by the group to make ends meet at the ranch. We did have our car. Fortunately, our family and friends were supportive and helped us with cash and furniture. That in itself was amazing. During our time in the cult, we had written letters "taking stands" with everyone important to us. This consisted of pointing out all the sin in their lives and threatening them with the fires of hell if they didn't change their ways and follow Christ in the uncompromising way we were. I think I wrote everyone—my aunts and uncles, parents, dear friends. At the time, I believed it was important to take these stands with everyone who was important to me. Robert misused Matthew 10:34–36:

> *Do not think that I came to bring peace on earth. I did not come to bring peace but a sword. For I have come to set a man against his father, a daughter, against her mother, and a daughter-in-law against her mother-in law, and a man's enemies will be those of his own household.*

Taking stands against friends and family members was an effective way of isolating us from everyone we had known. But when we were out, everyone came forth with love and support. They didn't press us for details, though I'm sure they wanted to know all that had transpired. We weren't ready to speak of it; the wounds were still too raw. When I see photos of myself from that time period, I see a dazed and empty look in my eyes.

Dan had remained in the group for a few months after I left. The ministry had lost the ranch. Robert had put it up as collateral for attorney's fees, but it also had a previous lien on it, so the attorneys got nothing. It reverted to the former owner.

Robert, Jane, Dan, and Christine moved to Palm Springs and got apartments there. Since my departure, Christine had been under constant scrutiny. Robert continuously attacked her relationship with me. Whenever he perceived she was "struggling," he'd flip her a quarter and say, "Why don't you go call your mom." I sent her some new clothes, and she felt she had to destroy them in order to prove her fidelity to Robert and the ministry. You didn't have to know you were struggling for these attacks to take place—it was Robert's way of keeping you off balance. Like the rats in B. F. Skinner's behaviorist experiments, cult members didn't know if they'd get a pellet of food or a shock from moment to moment.

I still don't know all that transpired during Dan and Christine's time in Palm Springs. Our family had not been able to speak completely frankly with one another about what we each experienced. But we had witnessed enough to know the searing pain the cult had brought into our lives. We knew each other to be profoundly broken.

Several months after I had left the Living Waters, Dan and Christine had come for a scheduled visit at my mom's house. The social worker, Marion Ulderman, was there. Dan would visit with Jason and I would visit with Christine. There were other cult members in the car with them—sent along for security, I'm sure—but Dan told Marion he did not want to return to the ministry. I was elated, but Christine was terrified. We all had been successfully convinced that departing from the ministry and returning to "the world" would be the ruination of us. Marion wisely offered Christine the opportunity to go to a "cool house" for a night or two, and she chose to do so. I am forever in Marion's debt. Years later I tried to find her so I could tell her of the children's progress and express my gratitude for her wisdom and kindness in handling our case, but I was unable to do so.

    We stayed with my mom and her husband for about six months. It was stressful for everyone. All of us were recovering from the trauma and still shifting in and out of the cult's teachings. Disbelief, fear, and regret were our daily portion. The easiest thing to do was to put our exterior lives together. We got the kids back in school—they were able to resume at the appropriate grades, even though they had missed a year of school. Dan and I went to the Back to School Night at the junior high where Christine was set to attend. On the spur of the moment, Dan spoke to the principal about a teaching job and was hired immediately—that was huge. I found a job at a nearby nursery school, and there the four of us were—either in school or employed. We were able to get our own apartment by Christmas. The outer shell was glued together.

fourteen

Recovery

It has taken me more than three decades to recover from our twenty-two-month stay at the Living Waters. I have done medicine walks, rounds of therapy, and energy healing. I've taken antidepressants. As my present husband, Christopher, says, I really got my mind blown. He's right.

But here is the miracle of all this suffering. God met me at every step of the way. And this is why I am convinced of His enduring love. He met me where I was, not in some prescribed place I "should" have been after the experience. I could no longer embrace formal Christianity, and for a while I couldn't embrace any spiritual practice, but gradually I regained a connection to "Spirit." I vowed to run like hell if I ever felt anything amiss in a group—to figure it out from a distance rather than trying to figure it out while remaining in it.

For a while, our family went to a Christian counselor who was specializing in cult recovery—as I mentioned, cults were big at the time. We did not go through deprogramming. Dan and I spoke about our cult experience at a seminar for religious educators. I remember a woman wanted us to do a radio show, and I told her that if what she wanted her audience to hear was that we were all recovered in Christ, she'd have to look elsewhere, because that certainly wasn't the case.

A lot of energy in those first years was spent just putting our physical lives together. Dan and I eventually divorced as we resumed old behavior patterns. I really didn't hold anything that had happened during the cult against him, the whole experience had been an aberration, but I didn't want to spend another fifteen years like the first fifteen years of our marriage. I thought that if I were going to hell for getting a divorce, I would just as soon go. The wounds were raw and I was spent.

Dan and I were able to work out an amicable settlement. We had nothing, so there was no property to fight over. We used a single attorney and established the amount of child support based on what a book said his salary would enable him to pay. He worked where Christine attended school, and I had started to work at the elementary school Jason attended. Dan saw the children regularly. I went back to college, which had been a lifelong dream, so while it was a struggle, it was also one of the happiest times for me. I had three jobs. We got two college students for roommates, I made meals in the slow cooker, and evenings would find us all studying at the dining room table. When I look back, I don't know how we did it all, but we did. I graduated from college, Christine graduated from high school, and Jason graduated from middle school in the same year. It felt like a triumph, and it was.

In case this sounds too idyllic, let me say there were times fraught with stress and confusion as we each struggled in our own way to recover. Reestablishing our lives in a new environment, paying off debt, and keeping our heads above water took all our energy. After once living in a lovely suburban home in Orange County, we were now in a tired apartment, but we were more than surviving. Though Dan and I were no longer married, the children excelled at school and were involved in theater productions and honors groups. I was winning awards at college, and Dan was extremely well liked and respected at his school. The walls of the house were going up.

fifteen
Restoration

While the practical necessities of living kept us occupied, the inner life was not so easily healed; in fact, it was put on the back burner. When I was directing a dance program at a theater arts magnet in the LA area, I hit a wall. The job was stressful, with multiple shows and long rehearsals. The students were bused in from areas all over Los Angeles, and they came with many needs. In any event, I reached the end of my resources. I was depressed and found it difficult to go to work. I called a therapist who had been recommended by a dear friend. When she picked up the phone and I introduced myself, I said, "I hate myself; can you fix it?"

My anger at God for allowing the cult experience, and my anger at Robert for all that had occurred had morphed into extreme self-loathing. I felt completely responsible for all that had happened, and I could not forgive myself for betraying the children. No amount of personal success or achievement and no amount of clear demonstration that the kids were doing well could convince me that I was OK. I no longer felt like a victim; I felt like the perpetrator.

My therapist, Barbara, and I worked on many aspects of my history. We looked at my family of origin. She recommended John Bradshaw's books to me, and I devoured them. We looked at my marriage and all the dynamics there, and we reviewed the events that occurred when I was in the cult. All of these things provided me with an understanding of how I had arrived where I was. I was able to come to some understanding of and have compassion for the wounded child I was inside. I decided to try and take care of that tender person, but I must say the shackles did not fall away. Barbara asked me, "When will you let yourself out of jail?" I couldn't say. Though I had gained some understanding, I did not possess the key to unlock the prison door.

A significant healing event took place on a Good Friday twenty years after I had left the cult. I had been able to return to Christian services and I had settled back into Catholicism, the tradition I had been raised in. On Good Friday, a large cross is passed through the congregation and everyone touches it. Previously I had always thought that Christ's sacrifice to atone for sin was for murderers and rapists, Hitler, Charles Manson—you know, for the "big sins"—not really for me personally. It occurred to me in a flash that Christ's death covered the cult. It was personal. It covered the children, it covered that horrible event, and it promised forgiveness. It gave me hope that my family could actually be healed.

That was a turning point for me, and I was able to begin dancing again. I returned to the Amazing Grace Dance Theater and was able to praise and worship God through movement. The experience of being welcomed back and accepted by the group, in fact, being honored by them, further restored my soul.

Time passed, and the exterior of my life moved forward as well. I remarried and the children progressed into adulthood, completed college, and established satisfying and meaningful careers: Christine, as an artist and professor; Jason, as a performing artist and drama teacher. Clearly, the kids were well, but I could not shake my guilt and shame. I had performed many rituals to "cleanse" myself of my cult experience. When I was in my Native American period, I had travelled with a friend to Ash Fork. I found a medicine wheel already there (I had planned to build one). I burned Robert's tapes and book. When restored to Catholicism, I made a complete confession—twice. I wrote. On dance retreats, experiences spilled out. I placed things on the altar, and I tried relentlessly to rid myself of the memories and shame of the cult. I made some progress and was able to function remarkably well. I think this made me wonder about the kids as well—were they highly functioning but crippled inside in some way? When I would ask them, they would assure me they were fine, that they didn't carry the painful memories of the cult in the same way I did. It was difficult for me to trust what they said, though, because I knew that they were aware of and sensitive to the burden of guilt I bore. When we did attempt the discussion of cult events, I would generally dissolve into tears. I regret that I was not able to be fully present to their processing of the experience due to my own emotional pain and sense of responsibility. Fortunately, they had friends who were.

The cult remained a shadow over me. I noticed certain sensitivities. I could not bear sharp or angry voices. They made me nervous. I frequently wondered if people were mad at me, though I could think of no reason why they would be. (I had often been taken by surprise in the cult when I would get in trouble, being unaware that I was doing anything wrong.) Any display of temper by significant people in my life would send me reeling. I was afraid of displeasing anyone in authority or anyone I cared about, and I hated the fear inside me. I was especially sensitive to any displeasure displayed by my husband, Christopher, who was similar in stature to Robert and to my father. I would ask myself, "What am I, seven? What am I so afraid of?" Though I generally acted independently, I was cringing inside—why?

When my husband and I retired and moved out of state these feelings intensified. I had not wanted to leave California and I didn't want to live so far away from my children, even though I knew it would be more affordable and I liked the city we settled in. I felt I had no choice; that my life was once again, out of my control. I felt I had abandoned my children again (even though they were now in their forties). Part of this was due to my understanding, or rather, my misunderstanding, of the role of a good wife. Somehow I felt I had no rights. When this move was in the works, I had prayed and asked God if this was the right move for us, and I did feel a "yes," but still I could not accept it. I felt as if I was in the cult again and as if my husband was a big man with a big club.

On my morning walks along the river, I could feel a gentle nudging in my awareness that my perceptions were skewed, but I could not shake the feeling that the cult experience was being repeated. I started sinking into a depression, and though I would not have planned to hurt myself, I knew that I felt it didn't matter if I went on living. Having experienced these thoughts once before, the first time I sought counseling, I knew they were a red flag. I was finishing up some routine medical checkups, and decided that if there were no physical causes for my depression, I would seek counsel. I had been in Idaho a year, had activities and new people I enjoyed, had travelled to California to see family and friends, and had visits from the children, but still my mental/emotional state was worsening.

Tearfully, I described my feelings to the doctor; she recommended an antidepressant and a psychologist. Almost immediately after I started the medication, my perspective shifted. I realized that I had probably been somewhat depressed for years and that my perspective on my husband was inaccurate. I had been diagnosed several years earlier with posttraumatic stress disorder, but I had not even considered this as the cause of my emotional state. The move and the dramatic change in my life had triggered these familiar feelings, and I became aware that I had what John Gottman refers to as an "enduring vulnerability." Any harshness in tone of voice, whether the anger was directed at me or at a situation in general, would trigger these flashbacks and intrusive memories of the cult. I would feel panicked and afraid, short of breath, disoriented. This vulnerability had been established in childhood, but reinforced in my marriage and through the cult. I was able to communicate this to my husband, who was not unaware of my history. But this time, I was able to identify my vulnerability to loud or harsh voices and facial expressions as my issue, not necessarily a flaw in Christopher. He is a person who loves discussion and debate and is passionate in his views. His way of expressing himself was triggering these reactions. I was able to say, "This is a vulnerability I have and I need you to be sensitive to it." I am now less afraid to talk to him about things and I can see his kindness and consideration. I won't say I am completely healed in this area, but I'm making progress—we're making progress together.

So how does this fit into my perception of God and His will? I understand now that no problem is merely spiritual. Prayer is effective, and effective prayer can lead to right action. There are physical, emotional, and psychological aspects to problems. God is always offering healing and restoration through countless forms: medical treatment, counseling, energy work, friends and strangers, nature, exercise, pets. His healing power is everywhere. I also learned that if I were going to be depressed and feel that life wasn't worth living, my body would start to cooperate with my desire to stop living. Each one of the medical tests I was having had to be repeated. Indicators of cancer and heart disease were identified, though follow-ups proved them false. Still, it was a wake-up call for me. Protect and honor your life, honor your spirit, honor your voice. When I say that God healed me, I mean He guided me through every step of recovery and to each resource that contributed to my healing. He will do the same for you.

I see that the children really are fine. They are happy and doing well, they don't need me to take care of them. Whatever scars they have, they address them as they present themselves. They have moved on. It's time for me to move on as well.

It is known in PTSD literature that if a person feels responsible for the trauma, it is harder for that person to get over it. Since my psychologist is also an art therapist, she suggested I draw some pictures. I drew a picture of myself in chains; on the side of my self-portrait is a larger drawing of a hand holding a key. I know the message is I have the key to unlock the shackles—but what is it? A decision? Self-love? Forgiving myself? I thought I had tried all those things.

No, the key was not only in forgiving, loving and accepting myself, but in recognizing the truth that my children have not been destroyed or defeated, that I have not been destroyed or defeated, —that in me, Christ has overcome the evil of the world, the sin and human foibles alike. That healing and restoration are available to everyone, no matter the gravity of the error. All things do work together for good for those who love the Lord and are called according to His purpose—and we're all called. The beatitudes took on new meaning for me as I saw the promise of His healing power in the words of Matthew 5:3–12:

Blessed are the poor in spirit,
For theirs is the kingdom of heaven

Blessed are they who mourn,
For they shall be comforted

Blessed are the meek,
For they shall possess the earth

Blessed are they who hunger and thirst for justice,
For they shall be satisfied.

Blessed are the merciful,
For they shall obtain mercy.

Blessed are the pure of heart,
For they shall see God.

Blessed are the peacemakers,
For they shall be called the sons of God.

Blessed are they who suffer persecution for justice sake,
For theirs is the kingdom of heaven.

God is not encouraging us to be downtrodden; He's saying that we have the victory no matter what condition we find ourselves in. No darkness or personal weakness can overcome us. His healing is everywhere. We hold the key to it. We must take action. Action may include returning to school, getting a therapist, seeing a doctor, taking medication—all of it will involve retraining our minds, because it is our habitual beliefs and mental patterns that either limit or free us. The universe will support us as we step out in faith, determination, and kindness. God wants us free and empowered. We must decide to be free and empowered and do the work it requires.

sixteen

Dan, Jason, and Christine

When Dan passed away a few years ago, from complications related to alcoholism, I was there to help the children take care of him: getting his home cleaned, bringing in meals, shopping for groceries. My brother-in-law found it strange that after so many years of estrangement, I would be there, cleaning and pitching in. I understand his confusion, but my journey had taught me that no matter what, in the end, there is only love. No heartache, hurt, or resentment could destroy the connection that Dan and I ultimately shared. The children and our experiences had forged our hearts together, though our lives were lived separately. During his last days, we had a few quiet moments alone. I said, "Dan, I'm so sorry I got us involved with that cult." And he replied, "And I'm sorry for everything that led up to it, that made you feel it was the only course to take." I felt at peace; I knew he understood, and I knew we had both forgiven each other.

Recently, I had a talk with Jason about what I was learning regarding the latest reoccurrence of my cult memories and feelings. I shared with him the insights I had gotten through Gottman's book *Relationship Rescue* about emotional philosophies in families and the enduring vulnerabilities they created. We talked about my parents and his dad, and about how Dan and I had parented Jason and Christine apart from the cult. I was happy to learn he considered me a "coach" in terms of dealing with life and emotions.

I expressed my concern about whether or not he had completely processed his experience in the cult and whether unaddressed wounds would cloud his judgments in relationships and other life decisions. I also expressed the idea that I was aware that he and Christine had not been able to process their experiences with me, because they were sensitive to the degree I was overcome with remorse, guilt, and shame, and so might underplay the lasting impact the cult had on them. Jason said he wasn't resistant to discussing these things with me; he just didn't want the conversation to lead to the place where I was asking for his forgiveness again. He said he harbored no resentment toward his dad or me regarding the experience.

Then he said something that made happiness and a lightness bubble up inside me. He said,
"Mom, for you, it would be like going to a doctor and him telling you that you had cancer and were going to die. That experience would be painful for you, you'd feel afraid, isolated, confused. Then after two years, another doctor and his team of doctors comes in and tells you you're not dying—you're not even sick—there's nothing wrong with you! You're terrific. You're awesome! Those two years would have been horrible for you, but the present predominant feeling would be one of relief and happiness—you're well."

It helped me immeasurably to know that Jason sees his time in the cult as a temporary misdiagnosis. It did not leave a permanent psychic wound—in fact, he tells me the pain he endured in this period has given him a depth of experience and emotion to draw from in his theater work—writing, acting, directing, and teaching. Go figure.

In the past thirty years I have often thought about writing a book about the cult. I thought it would be interesting to tell the story from each of our perspectives. What we each saw happening and what our true thoughts and feelings were at the time. I started and stopped many times. Recently I asked Christine if she would want to participate in a project like that since these memories were surfacing again for me. She is happily engaged in her own life and work, and said, "What would be the use of dredging all that up again?" For me, this has been an act of vomiting it all out on the page. PTSD literature says that if the memories and feelings continue to linger, then they haven't been completely processed yet.

Christine and Jason were victimized and abused. Their abuse took different forms. But both of them have gone on to get advanced degrees and have thriving careers. They have established meaningful and satisfying relationships. They are intelligent, generous, and kind. Each of us has scars, but we were not destroyed by them. Perhaps they have shaped us into better people; kinder, wiser, more compassionate.

seventeen

Healing Tools

I added this chapter five months after originally writing the manuscript. The memories wrote themselves. I would rise early and know I was to sit at the computer and begin. That content had been incubating for a long time. But getting it all out wasn't the final step in healing.

I had underestimated the diagnosis of PTSD. I knew that it was an anxiety disorder caused by a traumatic event. I knew that people could suffer flashbacks and inappropriate or over sensitized reactions to events that reminded them of, or were similar to, the original trauma. I was not aware, however, of what all the symptoms might be, or the variety of tools one could use to address the symptoms as well as the cause. I was in a hurry to get over the cult, get on with my life—this, too, is a very normal response in PTSD, but healing from PTSD is an ongoing process. It includes not just purging oneself of memories and experiences, but retraining the mind and emotions. It involves embracing oneself with ultimate compassion and patience as wounds are revealed and healed. The process cannot be hurried. It's like trying to get snow off your driveway after it has been driven on, melted a bit, and refrozen. It requires patiently chipping away at the edges, removing the surface layers of snow and waiting for the bottom level of ice to melt away or give way to the chipping, revealing the smooth, clear concrete below. There are many choices for treatment. All of them are beautifully detailed in Dr. Glenn R. Schiraldi's *The Post Traumatic Stress Disorder Sourcebook*, second edition.

I had not picked up this book until I retired and moved; further, I had not finished reading it when I wrote my memories and had started a few of the practices I learned in Karol Truman's and Louise Hay's books. I was sick of the cult, and I was impatient with myself for being "stuck" in the memories of it for so many years. Had I been treated for posttraumatic stress disorder on my initial visit to a psychotherapist, I may have recovered sooner. I had done some of the memory work, but none of the follow-up. As I read Dr. Schiraldi's book, I felt as if all of the puzzle pieces were falling into place. All my thoughts, symptoms, and reactions were described on the pages. He even used the "Humpty Dumpty" nursery rhyme to describe how a person with PTSD feels after the traumatic event. I saw my over serious and self-deprecating self reflected on the pages. I was surprised, humbled, and grateful. I had been dealing with something I had no understanding of. The therapists who had helped me had had parts of the puzzle, but none had had a complete understanding of PTSD and its treatment. And why should they have? PTSD is a diagnosis primarily given to war veterans, and its symptoms are recognized and treated mostly among that population, though this is changing.

I learned it is not enough to gain understanding about what circumstances and beliefs were causal in creating negative experiences—those beliefs and habitual thinking patterns need to be replaced. The first step is awareness. What is it I'm feeling? What am I thinking? Becoming the observer of emotions and thoughts as they arise and allowing them to pass through the mind and body is required. So, too, is noticing where in the body these feelings are experienced and identifying the belief that supports them. Then new thoughts must replace the old and habitual thoughts. Karol Truman's script and Louise Hay's practice of affirmations are especially helpful for "rewiring" the brain.

The Post Traumatic Stress Sourcebook points out that in addition to having the intruding memories and painful emotional reactions to situations that trigger them, the PTSD sufferer develops fear about experiencing these memories. This leads to the person avoiding the processing that would bring healing. I came to recognize that I was shielding myself from familiar and terrifying feelings by blocking out anything that might elicit a "negative" emotion. Like the monkeys, "Hear No Evil, See No Evil, and Speak No Evil," I refused to observe in order to block and manage painful emotions. I found the world and national news mostly depressing, and any discussion that became somewhat heated caused me to shut down. Since my husband, Christopher loved this kind of debate; it was very frustrating for him. I had spent over thirty years shutting down to manage my symptoms.

Recognizing that these were normal responses for a person who had experienced the kind of trauma I had was key and helped considerably. I am still coming to learn that emotions, like everything else, will pass and that I don't need to be afraid of or feel overwhelmed by them. I am allowing them to arise and dissipate using some of the mindfulness techniques of iRest, a modern meditation practice based on Yoga Nidra, and other strategies outlined in the *Post Traumatic Stress Disorder Sourcebook*. I am allowing, rather than resisting negative feelings. "This too shall pass" has become an effective mantra for me. In PTSD the nervous system has become over sensitized, and it takes conscious practice to calm it. It is a true chemical and physical condition that requires specific treatment.

The other side of dealing with uncomfortable feelings was setting clear limits. By respecting my condition, I learned that it was appropriate for me to protect myself from overwhelming situations. If I could feel my anxiety or avoidance escalating, it was my job to end the conversation for the time being. It would be in my best interest to resume the conversation when the traumatic feelings were not being activated. Walking away from negative interactions was not easy for me since I had never been good at setting limits and wanted to avoid confrontation at all costs. I began to see that setting limits was critical for my recovery though, and this was perhaps the most threatening aspect of my treatment. I had always been pretty good at doing what I needed to do internally to accept suffering, taking responsibility for my feelings and trying to give myself an attitude adjustment, looking for the positive in any difficult situation or person. Now I understood that I could withdraw from persons and situations (my response of choice) or confront (without attacking) the behaviors in others that were triggering me. I had a right to be spoken to respectfully and kindly. I had a right to initiate conversations or postpone them if they became anxiety arousing. I could deal with my symptoms and still engage meaningfully with the world.

This coping strategy is still all very new to me. I have to learn to communicate all over again. Being concerned with my feelings first, as a way to ensure my own recovery, I have to take the risk of a disagreement, judgment, or rejection from people who are the most significant to me. It's challenging to risk rejection, but I know I won't be fully functioning until I do, and I want to be fully functioning.

So, that's my story. If the reader finds any help in it, I'm glad. I will never again say, "OK, that's it; I'm done with it (the cult/PTSD) now." I realize that awareness and retraining my mind and behavior patterns will be a process and will take time, but I don't need to fear the process. My healing is inevitable because I desire it and take action to accomplish it. The universe supports me in both my desire and my action, and so I will succeed. I am determined to honor myself and treat myself and others with compassion during the process.

May you be happy.
May you be well.
May your life unfold with joy and ease.
May you be free.

Loving Kindness Meditation

eighteen

The Empowering and Transformational Practice of Prayer, Meditation and Yoga

The Kingdom of Heaven is within.
—*Jesus*

Practice and all is coming.
—*Pattabhijois*

It would be lovely if understanding our past and becoming aware of behavior patterns, conditioned beliefs, and attitudes would automatically change them. However, this is not the case. The task of retraining the mind and emotions takes time and energy. It involves every aspect of the human being: the physical structure, mental focus, and emotional balance. Yoga is a perfect tool for addressing all these aspects.

Christians are often reluctant to practice yoga. There is a fear that yoga is a religion, that they will be worshipping "false gods." I have felt this apprehension myself. However, I have discovered that there is no conflict between the practice of yoga and the teachings of Christ. In fact, the Yamas and the

Niyamas, which are the ethical principles of yoga, are the same teachings contained in the Gospel of Christ and in the Ten Commandments. Further, I have found that these principles of yoga can expand and enhance our understanding of these Christian teachings.

The physical practice of yoga requires attention to the present moment. The sensations of the body, feelings, and thoughts are brought into awareness and observed without judgment. There is acceptance of the body, mind, and spirit just as it currently exists—exactly what Christ offered—acceptance, non-judgment, and forgiveness to all sinners, regardless of the sin. Yoga offers the practitioner practices that can be followed every day—physical poses that require strength and flexibility, patience, a daily practice. The qualities needed to enter and sustain these postures are the same qualities we need in life. Yoga offers concrete meditative strategies and instructions, which, when followed, will calm the mind and nervous system, reducing anxiety, so that we are able to follow Christ's instruction to "be anxious for nothing" (Philippians 4:6–7).

Yoga, in a few words, is a tool for uniting the body and mind with God, in whatever way you understand Him. It is compatible with Christianity, Buddhism, Taoism, Hinduism, etc. The principles of yoga—nonviolence, truth, non-excessiveness, contentment, gratitude, surrender, to list a few—are in complete agreement with the teachings of Christ. *The Yamas and the Niyamas* by Deborah Adele elucidates this point most clearly and will soothe the apprehensions of anyone questioning whether yoga is in conflict with his or her faith.

Of course, there are many physical benefits to yoga, and yoga can be approached and embraced on the physical level alone. But in my opinion, the true power of yoga is the access it gives us through the practice to enter the present moment and unite ourselves with the divine and begin to embody the characteristics we desire: joy, peace, patience, kindness, perseverance, faith, integrity, contentment, and compassion. There are many authors/teachers who express this very eloquently, and I have included their works in the bibliography to assist you in your desire for greater joy and freedom. Please browse through it and choose a title that resonates with you—Begin the journey.

May you have a day of infinite blessings and the vision to see them.
Debbie Murphy , McCall, Idaho

nineteen

Practice, Practice, Practice

"Start where you are, again and again"
—Pema Chödrön

Healing from trauma is an ongoing process. Be patient with yourself in every way and accept that this is a natural part of living. Above all, extend to yourself kindness and compassion in every circumstance. Oprah refers to it as "extreme self-care." The following are some practices that you may find helpful on your journey. Engage professional services to assist you as you deal with traumatic events that have been emotionally and physically damaging to you, especially if you are feeling overwhelmed with fear, anxiety, depression or self-hatred. The importance of this cannot be overstated. Feel free to use a variety of approaches, but find a professional who is familiar with the symptoms and attributes of PTSD.

Tell your story and share it with people who are important to you.

Reliving the past is not something that is beneficial unless it is a process by which you heal from damaging experiences.

Iyanla Vanzant refers to it as *soul surgery*. In her book "Until Today!" She says: "the most challenging part of the process is that you have to walk in the depths of all that you have done in order to heal it." So get it ALL out, the grief, the anger, the guilt, the shame, whatever memories haunt you - hold nothing back. I suggest doing this in written form, because just thinking about it can keep the thoughts rummaging around in your head without resolving and dissolving the experience. With no intention to blame or shame ourselves, we can often recognize thought and behavior patterns that contribute to our trauma. Karol Truman's book "Feelings Buried Alive Never Die" can be very helpful in processing these experiences and John Bradshaw's books on the Family and it's dysfunction will provide insight and understanding for many behavior patterns that are no longer serving you. Once you have written the fullness of your truth, share it with a few significant people. To be known and loved for all that we are and have experienced is essential to the human spirit. When you have processed the trauma completely, you will know because it will no longer haunt you, and it will be truly relegated to the past. Now release it.

Affirm Yourself

Louise Hay's "You Can Heal Your Life" is a wonderful resource for learning to value and affirm yourself. Habituated, negative self talk is very common. Start to become aware of the messages you give yourself regularly; "I'm fat", "I'm old, "that was stupid of me", "I'll never get this right", "I blew it". Don't judge yourself for having these thoughts, simply replace them and start each day with powerful statements about who you are. "I am capable", "I am worthy", "I am healthy", "and I am fearless". Louise Hay even suggests singing to yourself in the mirror. It may feel foolish at first, speaking these things that you don't quite believe, but gradually you will discover how these positive messages improve your emotional state and self concept. Another book I find especially helpful is Sharon Salzburg's "Loving Kindness, The Revolutionary Art of Happiness". In it, we are encouraged to extend kindness to ourselves first and then to others.

Quiet the Mind - Come into the Present Moment

The best way I know to come into the present moment when your mind and emotions are spinning, is to focus on your breath. Breathe in. Breathe out. Focus on the sensation of the air flowing into and out of your nostrils. Slow and expand the breath, this practice will also relax you. Scripture tells us *"Be still and know that I am God"* (Psalm 46:10). Only by becoming quiet can we access our divine nature and divine source. This, you will discover, will take a lot of practice. "Monkey Mind" is the term Buddha used to describe the human mind. We all have monkey minds, filled with chattering monkeys, screeching and clamoring for attention, carrying on endlessly. Meditation practices teach us to become a witness to these restless thoughts, and rather than follow them, allow them to pass through. Calming the mind this way, even for short periods of time, on a daily basis will assist you in gaining clarity and inner peace. Eckhart Tolle's "The Power of Now", and Max Strom's "A Life Worth Breathing" are illuminating.

Forgiveness

One of the most important practices in recovering from trauma is forgiveness. Hatred, anger, and resentment will damage you, while leaving their object untouched. If you cannot bring yourself to forgive a person or situation, set an intention to forgive them. Let God know you are willing to try to forgive. That is all that is needed for a heart change and your freedom. Equally important is forgiving the self. We all make mistakes, it is good to recognize our failings and forgive ourselves quickly and completely. This frees us to experience joy and peace rather than ruminate over the past. The more readily we can forgive ourselves, the easier it will be to forgive others. This is not easy, nor does it happen overnight. Accepting that personal transformation is a process will bring you more ease with difficult emotions.

Practice Gratitude

This can be very difficult when you are in the midst of a challenging and threatening situation, or when you are feeling hopeless and despairing. But turning the mind to things you are grateful for will change your emotional state. Perhaps to start with, it is merely a piece of fruit, a sunset, fresh air, or a dear pet. Begin with small things and gradually you will become aware of greater gifts. Make a practice of this - perhaps mentally listing 10 things each day for which you are grateful. Better yet, write them down. Then when you are having a particularly bad day (and you will), you can look at them and be reminded of the good in your life.

Meditation and Prayer

The daily quieting of the mind is perhaps the most important practice for transformation, that and prayer. Asking for clarity and wisdom, guidance in your plans and activities will bring peace. Asking God to bless what you have already decided to do will not necessarily create the life you want. Rather, seek

God's direction for your life, moment to moment. This may require slowing down a bit, waiting for an answer. Sometimes what our personality or ego wants is not what will best serve us, or the ones we love. Often times we are burdened with worry over a loved one. It might be an illness, a job loss, a rocky marriage, or an addiction. How does our fretting help that person or situation? Not only is it unhelpful, it disturbs our wellbeing by inducing anxiety and stress - all of which contribute to physical ailments. We're all familiar with the expression "I'm worried sick." The best thing we can do, as Iyanla Vanzant says in her book, "Until Today!" is roll it over to God. If you have no experience with meditation, videos, CDs and books abound with mediation practices, several included in the bibliography. There are resources on the Internet, many of them free. Find what works for you and make it a part of your daily routine.

Patience

Patience with yourself, with others, with circumstances, and with the process of recovering from trauma is essential. It is for this reason I included Pema Chodron's quote at the opening of this chapter. Greet yourself with kindness each day, no matter what condition you find yourself in, and begin again. Whatever occurs in your daily life, know that it will pass. Tomorrow will be different. Allowing everything to be as it is will provide inner peace and the quietude needed to discern appropriate action.

Move

Get moving! Exercise restores the mind as well as the body. But rather than thinking of it as drudgery, find a physical activity you enjoy doing. Walking, dancing, hiking, swimming, weight lifting, or playing a sport will get those endorphins flowing, create a more positive outlook and release tension. If you find yourself in nature while you are moving, that is even better, since nature is a great restorative. Yoga can be of great value because as stated previously, it develops strength, flexibility, balance, and encourages attention to the present moment. As you are moving, you are focused on the sensations you are experiencing in the body. It also incorporates breath work, which in itself can be meditative.

Find opportunities to do what you love

The pursuits you delight in are clues to recognize the gifts you have to give to the world. One of my favorite books is Sonia Choquette's "The Answer Is Simple, Love Yourself, Live your Spirit." It is one of the finest works I've read for helping people connect with their divine spirit and live lives of joy. Even if you are in a job you hate or feel stuck in, make time to pursue your passions. It may lead to different employment or it may simply provide moments of pleasure that will sustain and satisfy your soul. Reading, writing, painting, quilting, sewing, gardening - so many pleasures to pursue, better get started.

Acknowledgments

I want to thank all the friends and family members who prayed and acted for our deliverance from the Living Waters, including my parents and siblings, as well as Dan's parents and siblings. They, along with my friends Charlene, Stella, and Eileen, saw us through the nightmare and reached out in countless ways. I am grateful to my children and their father, Dan, who did the work necessary to recover and restore their own lives, and to the people who supported them throughout their journey: Matt, Lynlee, and their extended friends and family. I am grateful for Barbara Bear, the therapist who began to unlock the chains that bound me, and for subsequent therapists and health practitioners, Lester Summerfield, Tracy Morgan, Mariella Hogan, Jeanne Dillion, and Heather Doleigh. I'm grateful for the medication that enabled me to process this experience and for the yoga practices that helped me replace destructive thought patterns and beliefs with healthy and constructive ones. I thank every person who has listened sympathetically to portions of this tale and who continues to pray for my family's complete recovery. They have provided love and support for many years.

There are countless others—friends, acquaintances, teachers, supervisors—who by their lives helped to restore mine, whose friendship and affection validated and healed me. I particularly want to thank my husband, Christopher, who "dragged" me away from California, which provided me the opportunity to process the trauma I suffered, and who has suffered as the "trigger" for my PTSD.

I thank God for every gift under heaven: earth, sea, sky, art, music, people, pets, movement, and sunshine—all have contributed in making me whole again. You, God, are the air that I breathe, and I love you.

I wish to acknowledge Elizabeth Strout, an author I heard speak, who said that the stories we are ashamed of, embarrassed by, and are afraid we'll be rejected over are the stories that need to be told. I also want to acknowledge Anita Moorjani, author of *Dying to Be Me*. Her book was the wake-up call I needed to encourage me to put an end to my depression and start creating a life of happiness. *Feelings Buried Alive Never Die* by Karol K. Truman provided a useful script for healing and rewriting habitual thought patterns and beliefs, as did Louise Hay's classic *You Can Heal Your Life*. Eckhart Tolle's *The Power of Now* and *A New Earth,* as well as Brother Lawrence's *Practicing the Presence of God* provided insight for connecting with the divine and eternal love that is always available to us in the present moment, should we seek to access it.

I also wish to thank my editor, Susan, from Create Space, whose thoughtful comments helped bring clarity to my writing.

About the Author

Valerie Martin has a Masters degree in Educational Guidance and Counseling and is a certified yoga teacher. She is available for individual or group sessions and presentations. She can be contacted at: info@thequietpath.net

Bibliography

Adele, Deborah. *The Yamas and the Niyamas: Exploring Yoga's Ethical Practice.* Duluth, MN: On-Word Bound Books, 2009.

Bradshaw, John. *Healing the Shame That Binds You.* Deerfield Beach, FL: Health Communications, 2005.

Bradshaw, John. *The Family: A New Way of Creating Solid Self-Esteem.* Deerfield Beach, FL: Health Communications, 1996.

Chödrön, Pema. *Comfortable with Uncertainty.* Boston, MA: Shambhala Publications, Inc, 2003.

Choquette, Sonia. *The Answer is Simple, Love Yourself, Live Your Spirit,* Carlsbad, CA: Hay House, 2008.

Dillion, Jeanne. *iRest® in Serenity, Finding Peace in a Chaotic World: Yoga Nidra with Jeanne Dillion.* Boise, ID: Yoga for Wellness LLC, 2013. MP3 or CD-ROM.

Emerson, David, and Hopper, Elizabeth. *Overcoming Trauma through Yoga: Reclaiming Your Body.* Berkley, CA: North Atlantic Books, 1973.

Forbes, Bo. *Yoga for Emotional Balance: Simple Practices to Relieve Anxiety and Depression.* Boston: Shambhala, 2011.

Germer, Christopher K. *The Mindful Path to Self-Compassion: Freeing Yourself from Destructive Thoughts and Emotions.* New York: Guilford Press, 2009.

Gottman, John M., and DeClaire, Joan. *The Relationship Cure.* New York: Three Trees Press, 2001.

Hay, Louise L., *You Can Heal Your Life.* Carlsbad, CA: Hay House, 1999.

Lucado, Max. *Just Like Jesus.* Nashville, TN: W Publishing Group, 2003.

Miller, Richard. *Yoga Nidra: A Meditative Practice for Deep Relaxation and Healing.* Boulder, CO: Sounds True, 2010.

Moorjani, Anita. *Dying to Be Me.* Carlsbad, CA: Hay House, 2012.

Peck, M. Scott. *The Road Less Traveled: A New Psychology of Love, Traditional Values, and Spiritual Growth.* New York: Simon and Schuster, 1978.

Salzburg, Sharon. *Loving-Kindness: The Revolutionary Art of Happiness.* Boston: Shambhala, 2002.

Salzburg, Sharon. *Real Happiness: The Power of Meditation, A 28-Day Program.* New York: Workman Publishing, 2011.

Santa, Thomas M. "Scrupulosity and How to Overcome It." CatholicCulture.org. http://www.catholicculture.org/culture/library/view.cfm?recnum=3739.

Schiffmann, Erich. *The Art of Moving into Stillness.* New York: Pocket Books, 1996.

Schiraldi, Glenn R. *The Post Traumatic Stress Disorder Sourcebook: A Guide to Healing, Recovery, and Growth.* New York: McGraw Hill, 2009.

Stearns, Mary Nurrie, and Stearns, Rick Nurrie. *Yoga for Anxiety: Meditations and Practices for Calming the Body and Mind.* Oakland, CA: New Harbinger Publications, 2010.

Strom, Max. *A Life Worth Breathing.* New York: Skyhorse Publishing, 2012

Tolle, Eckhart. *A New Earth: Awakening to Your Life's Purpose.* Vancouver, BC: Namaste Publishing, 2005.

Tolle, Eckhart. *The Power of Now.* Novato, CA: New World Library, 1999.

Truman, Karol K. *Feelings Buried Alive Never Die.* St. George, UT: Olympus Distributing, 2003.

Vanzant, Iyanla. *Until Today! Daily Devotions for Spiritual Growth and Peace of Mind,* New York: Fireside, 2000.

Weaver, Joanna. *Having a Mary Heart in a Martha World.* Colorado Springs, CO: Waterbrook Press, 2004.

White, Ganga. *Yoga Beyond Belief: Insights to Awaken and Deepen Your Practice.* Berkley, CA: North Atlantic Books, 2007.

Printed in Great Britain
by Amazon

61682903R20057